CraftMaker

ULTIMATE

ROCK PAINTING

hinkler

Katie Cameron

hinkler

Published by Hinkler Books Pty Ltd
45–55 Fairchild Street
Heatherton Victoria 3202 Australia
www.hinkler.com

Author: Kate Cameron
Cover design: Sam Grimmer

ISBN: 978 1 4889 1974 9

Printed and bound in China

Contents

Getting Started

Want your artistry to shine? Rock art is one of the most ancient forms of artistic expression known to humans, and making rock art is increasing in popularity as a creative pastime.

Using metallic paint is a fantastic way to add a brilliant shine to your works of rock art, highlighting and adding a fun, eye-catching glimmer. Or why not brighten up your home or garden with some dazzling neon pieces, or light up a friend's day with a gorgeous glow-in-the dark gift?

There are 18 wonderful rock-painting activities in this book, including bold but simple designs, intricate geometric arrangements, awe-inspiring mandalas, cute character pieces, and much more. Many of the designs draw on the natural world, taking their inspiration from the sea, land, sky, and beyond. There are even a few fantastical designs to help your imagination run wild!

You don't need to be a skilled painter to create these colorful artworks—anyone can do it! Creating painted rocks can be a fun and fulfilling way to spend a few hours. Take your creations to the next level and really make your rocks stand out with shining metallics, vibrant neons, and fabulous phosphorescents!

Stones

The best kinds of stones to paint on are smooth and free of cracks or holes. If a stone has a bumpy surface, painting can be problematic and clean-line details are difficult to achieve.

If you are going to gather your own stones, smooth stones are most commonly found along the shores of oceans and fast-moving rivers. If this is not an option, or if you want to save time, smooth stones can also be purchased from craft stores. Keep in mind that the larger the stone, the longer it can take to complete.

Be sure to thoroughly clean all your rocks before you start. Rinse off the bulk of any mud or sand outside (not down the kitchen drain, or it can get blocked), and then give them a scrub in the sink with soap and water. Leave them to air dry in a sunny location, such as a windowsill. Ensure the stones are free from any dust or debris and are completely dry before you begin.

IMPORTANT:
Make sure it's OK to take the stones from your area. Some places have regulations to protect the environment against things such as erosion or risks to animal habitat, and in some places it can be culturally inappropriate to remove stones. Ensure that you always ask permission if taking from private property.

If you can't find the perfect stone for the design you want to paint, try forming your own "rocks" using store-bought polymer clay.

Paints

Acrylic craft paint works very well for painting stones. It is non-toxic, fast drying, and adheres well to a stone's surface. It is affordable, easy to clean up, and simple to remove from brushes with a little soap and water.

Drying time can range from less than 5 minutes up to 15 minutes, or more. This is affected by several factors, including how thickly the paint is applied, temperature, and humidity. It can take up to 24 hours for acrylic paint to "cure" to the point that it is completely dry and at maximum hardness. It's important not to touch the stone during this time or you risk smudging it or leaving fingerprints.

HaNDY HINT

Have the paint colors you plan to use, or have been using, set aside. This comes in handy if you are mixing a new shade, picking up where you left off, or if you are applying a second coat. You don't want to apply a second coat in the wrong color!

Metallic Paints

Metallic acrylic craft paints share the same great qualities as regular craft paint and are a great addition to your art supplies. With metallic, you can add a delightful shimmer to just about all your craft or home décor projects. It is especially fabulous when painting on stone because, just like regular paint, it dries quickly and has good coverage. Metallic acrylic craft paint is water-based, making clean-up easy with a little soap and water. It is durable, and will keep its shine even if used with outdoor crafts.

Painting with metallics is much the same as with regular paint, but there are a few differences you'll want to keep in mind. One problem you may run into is your brush strokes showing up visibly on your design, which is due to the shiny mineral pigment that metallic paint is made from. A stroke that is made from the left to the right can look different to a stroke that is made from right to left, so make your stone look more consistent by always painting in the same direction. Don't overload the paint on your soft-bristled brush or press down too hard on your brush while painting with metallic paints.

Paint your details first then smooth over with any further coats. Apply thin coats and reload your brush often. Try to work quickly, if possible, painting in shorter strokes. Then go back and lightly drag the brush from one end of the stone to the other, always in the same direction. This will smooth out lines while you paint.

You may find that your stones develop ridges in your once smooth painted surface. This is usually because there wasn't sufficient time for the first coat to dry before adding the next. The new coat pulled the layer below that wasn't quite dry along with it and no amount of additional coats will get you out of that mess. To fix this, it's best to make sure you allow the paint to fully dry, then use a fine sandpaper to sand down the bumps. Wipe away the dust and start again.

Keep in mind that smudges and fingerprints are also particularly cumbersome to fix with metallic paint because its gleam attracts attention.

With metallic paints, you can mix them together to create some fun new colors, or mix metallic with regular paint for a shiny new shade. Some combinations of metallic mix-ups are:

gold + metallic blue = golden green
gold + metallic purple = rose gold
silver + gold = bronze
red + gold = copper

plus many more dazzling combinations!

If you find yourself without a color of metallic paint that you really need, you can actually make your own metallic paint colors by adding silver or white pearl paint (or mica-based eyeshadow since many metallic paints get their shine from the mineral mica!) to a regular matte shade you have on hand. It's best to experiment with any DIY metallic paint mix-ups and "hacks" before beginning painting on stone.

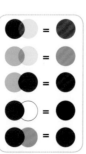

Neon Paints

Regular colors absorb light while neon absorbs and reemits it, causing it to appear bright.

Be aware that neon acrylic colors are not alike across all brands. The intensity of the color varies, as does the opacity. In general, neon colors are translucent. Regular acrylic paint is largely opaque, meaning it will apply in one or two coats without being see-through. Neon paints require several coats to appear intense in color and so that you cannot see what is beneath.

Neon shades can be darkened with a little bit of black or lightened with a little white; however, you cannot make any new neon colors. Neon pigment is man-made and this brightness is generally limited to pink, orange, yellow, green, blue, and red colors. You can intermix neon paint with regular acrylic paint to make some interesting new shades; the brightness will be muted but will still yield some fun colors. Just don't expect to make a new neon!

Glow-in-the-Dark Paints

Glow-in-the-dark paint is also known as "phosphorescent paint," "luminous paint," or simply "glow paint." It's a type of paint that you can see in the dark (obviously!), and is created using man-made luminescent phosphors, such as zinc oxide or strontium aluminate. When you shine light on these chemicals, they absorb and store the light energy and then release it gradually.

Don't confuse glow paint with neon paint or fluorescent paint. Though these paints look very bright during daylight and will 'glow' under a UV blacklight, once all lights are out you won't be able to see them. Glow paint will glow under a UV light and will also visibly glow with no lights on at all. Glow paint won't glow forever without some recharging, of course! Just expose the paint to light (from a bright light bulb, a UV blacklight, or sunshine) to recharge it. The good news is that you can do this over and over—there's no limit to the amount of times you can recharge the paint. Your creations will always be ready to glow again, after they've been exposed to light!

Try out your glow paint before starting, as not all glow paint is the same. You'll want to test for things like thickness and opacity, so you can determine how much paint to put on your brush and how many layers you need to get a good glow on.

Glow paint tends to work best—that is, you need fewer coats and it looks brighter for longer—when it's applied over white or light-colored backgrounds.

Avoid uneven glow (caused by streaks or raised edges) by using less glow paint on your brush and applying thin coats, adding more as needed. Also, give your glow paint a little extra time to dry between coats: 10 to 15 minutes or more, depending on the thickness of the coat.

Don't mix glow paint with regular paint—this will reduce the glow effect when the lights are out. Regular acrylic paint is opaque and will block the light from charging the glow particles.

HANDY HINT

Speed up drying time between coats by using a hair dryer on a low setting.

Tools

There are a few tools that are useful when painting rocks:

- Pencil and eraser—use these to sketch out your ideas and designs on paper beforehand. Light graphite pencil markings can be used directly on the stone or dry paint, and an eraser can remove any marks, or you can simply paint over them.

- Drawing compass and ruler—you can use your eye to judge measurements like center points for designs and base coats, but a ruler and compass make this process much faster and easier. If symmetry is an important factor in your design, you will want precise and equal measurements on all sides. These tools are useful when forming new designs on paper. A compass may be difficult to use on some shapes of stones; if this is the case, use your judgement to visually choose the center spot.

- Paintbrushes—pointed brushes are best for fine detailing and lines, dotting and touch-ups. Use a larger-sized round or flat brush when painting areas that need more coverage (i.e. base coats). Generally, brushes with shorter handles and shorter, firmer bristles work better to achieve precise detailing. It is important to keep your brushes in good condition with the bristles straight and together. Never let brushes dry with paint on them, and only dip them into the paint to about half the hair length so the paint doesn't get on the ferrule (the little metal piece that attaches the bristles to brush handle). Getting paint on the ferrule will inevitably result in spreading and frayed bristles, no matter how much you wash your paintbrush. Have a little cup of water at your work station so that you can quickly wash off paint and keep brushes moist before washing them thoroughly with soap and water.

- Paint or permanent-ink pens—these can be a little expensive but even just having black and white in an extra or ultra-fine tip can be invaluable. Use them to outline your design and to create extra-fine details that need to be all the same size, which can be very frustrating to achieve using paint and a brush!

- Dotting stylus—also known as a nail dotting tool or embosser, this looks similar to a pencil. It has a needle in one or both ends and a small round ball on the tip. This handy little device can be found at craft stores; it is fairly inexpensive and is fantastic for dotting in acrylic paint. Another option is to use the pointed ends of household items. Think toothpicks, skewers, small dowels, unsharpened pencil ends, etc. These items allow precision and control when doing intricate dot work, and care is minimal as you do not have to clean them! You can allow the paint to dry on the sticks, which can layer and create new sizes for their ends; or you can pull off the dried paint and keep a small, pointed end.

HANDY HINT

If you're using dowels as dotting tools, you can sharpen them with a pencil sharpener or blade to create a variety of dotting sizes.

Applying a Clear Finish

Most craft stores stock affordable clear, gloss, or matte acrylic finishes that will make your colors appear brighter and seal them in place longer. It will also protect against fading, and make your stones resistant to water and weather conditions. The spray-on type is preferable to the brush-on type, as this is quick and easy, and adheres to all parts of the stone in a uniform, even manner.

Always wait until your stone is complete, the paint is completely dry and hard, and the stone is free of any dust or unwanted particles before spraying the protective finish in a well-ventilated room or outside. Allow at least a day for the finish to dry, then apply a second coat and allow it to dry again. As with paint, avoid touching your stone while the finish is drying to ensure the coating hardens smoothly.

Work Space

You will need a large, well-lit work station with enough space for you to paint and also have everything you need within arm's reach. Your station should be high enough to maintain good posture, and be equipped with a comfortable chair.

Painting these beautiful stones can take a lot of time, so be aware of the time you're spending and try not to sit for too long! Be sure to get up, stretch, and move around for ten minutes or so at least once an hour. Movement is good for your body's circulation and can also help you refocus.

To keep your work space neat and tidy, place a piece of cardboard or paper towel beneath your stone before you begin, and protect the remainder of your space with old newspaper. The cardboard helps to keep the underside of the stone clean and can also be helpful if you wish to move the stone to another area without needing to pick it up.

When you're using glow-in-the dark paint, it's helpful to have a bright desk lamp nearby to charge the glow paint. Having the on/off switch close by makes checking your work that much quicker in a dimly lit room.

Fixing Mistakes and Other Tips and Tricks

Here are a few other little tips that I'd like to share before you start your rock painting journey

- Be patient—painted rocks can take many hours, if not days, to complete. Patience is key. If you rush, you may make mistakes that could have been avoided. That being said, don't worry too much about tiny imperfections. In the grand scheme of things, they often go unnoticed in all the other details.

- Dot fix—dropped an uneven dot or made one so big it ran into the others? Depending on where and when in the process this happens, you may be able to wipe the paint away using some water and a brush, or scrape the mistake off with a stick, or some fine sandpaper. It is safer to allow the area (if not the entire stone) to dry before you try to fix mistakes. Clear away any flakes before repainting the area with the same color as the underlying coat. Allow the new paint to dry and reapply your dot. It's like it never happened!

- Acrylic "eraser"—the good thing about acrylic paint is that it is very thick so you can use it to paint over a mistake without the original paint showing through. The base color is your friend! Use it as an "eraser" for small mistakes. Don't like the dot color you have chosen? Dot right over the top of it. Voila!

- Wonky designs—if you didn't quite start in the middle and your design is off center, use more base paint to even out the circle, thus centering your design. If you have messed up more than it's worth taking the time to fix, scrub off the paint using soap and water. It is just a rock, after all!

Before You Begin

Here are a few tips before you start your rock-painting journey.

- Plan ahead—sketch out your design idea before you start. Trace the shape of your stone onto a piece of paper so you can get an idea what will fit on your "canvas." Use a ruler and drawing compass to practice making circles and other geometric shapes. It is helpful to get the hang of a pattern on paper before it's set on stone.

- Dot practice—practice, practice, practice! Precision with dots takes a steady hand and knowing how to place the brush or stick with just the right pressure. Dip your tool into the paint often to leave a thick, nicely saturated dot. This means that your dot is less likely to need a second coat of paint, and you are less likely to make a mistake. Try out different styles of dot art and practice making shapes and patterns. Before starting, use the dotting tool to do a test dot on some paper to get a feel for how the paint will transfer and what pressure is needed for an evenly shaped circular dot.

- Brush-stroke practice—brushes come in different sizes and shapes to create different paint strokes. Use a large flat brush to cover big areas and a small, round brush for details and outlines. Paint large areas or backgrounds first. Start with mid to bright colors and then add dark colors.

Dragon Egg

Just like the dragons from legends, you won't be able to help coveting and guarding this gorgeous rock once you create it. This makes the perfect ornament or the ideal gift, particularly for the fantasy fan in your life!

You will need:

- Oval or egg-shaped stone (2.5 in or 6 cm length)
- Pencil
- Fine-tip black permanent marker (or black paint)
- Paint: gray, black (optional)
- Metallic paint: green, dark green, blue, purple, gold
- Paintbrush: small, medium
- Dotting tools: small, medium, large
- Protective finish
- Small gems and adhesive (optional)

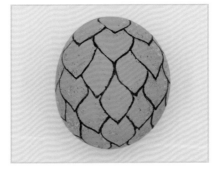

1 Paint the stone with a light-colored base (I have used gray paint). This means you'll need fewer coats of metallic paint. Using a fine-tip black marker or black paint and a small brush, draw rows of pointed scales to cover the stone from top to bottom. Make sure the scales are of an equal size.

2 Paint the entire stone with metallic green paint. (If you don't have green, you can mix gold and blue metallic paint). Refresh the black scale outline if needed.

3 Use a different shade of metallic green to add shading along the edges and corners of the scales where they overlap.

4 When the paint is dry, use a smaller brush to paint contrasting colors through the middle of each of the scales. Paint metallic blue through the center scales and metallic purple in the side scales. Leave a border of green along the edge of each scale. Once the paint has dried, paint a second coat and blend more into the green borders.

5 Refresh the black outlines around the scales and add decorative detailing: paint small gold dots along the edges of the scales and a line of larger dots running down the center of the stone. Remember to leave room if you plan to use gems or other ornaments. Spray your stone with protective finish.

6 Apply any additional gems or other mixed media once the stone has completely dried. Using tweezers helps to place them on the stone.

HANDY HINT

Decorate the egg with gemstones or other metallic decorative beads or sequins. Just remember to wait until after the stone has been coated with protective finish before gluing anything to the stone. Try using other mixed media to decorate the stone: you could use a hot glue gun on the stone and then paint over the glue when dry.

Sea Urchin

For this fun dot design reminiscent of those little ocean creatures, use neon paint to highlight regular paint colors. Choosing a circular stone adds to the symmetry of the design and mimics a sea-urchin shape; however, you can paint the design on just about any stone with enough flattened areas.

You will need:

- Stone
- Drawing compass (optional)
- Dotting tools: small, medium, large
- Paintbrushes: small, medium, large
- Paint: black, pink, yellow, bright blue or turquoise, yellow-orange, aqua, purple, light purple, light orange, mid-orange, dark orange, dark purple, red-orange, red
- Neon paint: yellow, orange, pink, green
- Protective finish

1 Use a drawing compass or sketch a base circle to cover most of the stone, leaving the edges exposed. With a larger round brush, fill in the circle with black paint. Allow to dry and, using pink paint and your dotting tool, place a dot in the center. Generally, regular craft paint is opaque enough that you can use one or two coats and not need to prime before using bright colors.

2 Using a smaller tool, place eight small white dots evenly around the center dot. Keep all dots apart from each other. In the small spaces between these white dots, closer to the pink dot, use your tool and a steady hand to place eight extra tiny dots. Continue on to the next ring of small dots, keeping them the same size as the white but using bright yellow paint. These dots are staggered, placed just below the spaces between the small white dots.

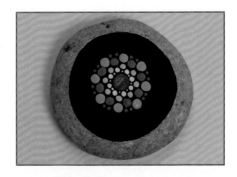

3 Paint a ring of staggered, slightly larger dots. Use bright blue or turquoise paint. Add the next ring of staggered dots using yellow-orange. Make these dots slightly larger again: 0.15 inches in diameter. These are slightly sunk into the spaces between the bright blue, without touching each other. In the space between the yellow-orange dots, just below the bright blue dots, place two small aqua dots side

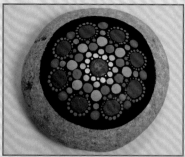

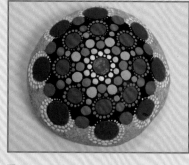

by side.

4 Directly below and aligned between these aqua dots, use a small brush or large dotting tool for purple-colored dots about 0.2 in (5 mm) in diameter. Space them out and add a ring of tiny light purple dots around each one. Make the dots in the ring taper down in size as you reach the aqua dots. In the space between the ringed purple dots, place a small light orange dot. Directly below, add another slightly larger mid-orange dot.

5 Between the orange dots and in line with the ringed purple dots, use a small brush and a deeper shade of purple to form slightly larger dots, leaving some space around them. Use your large dotting tool and dark orange paint to place dots about 0.2 in (5 mm) in between the dark purple dots. Use a small dotting tool to complete two tapered tiny dotted rings in white around the purple dots. End the second outermost white ring as you reach the dark orange dots.

6 Finish the rows of orange dots with a red-orange and a red dot, using whatever size will fit. Allow all paint to dry to touch for 15 minutes or so. All yellow, orange, and red dots should be in a relatively straight line out from the center, and all blue and purple dots should be in a straight line from the center.

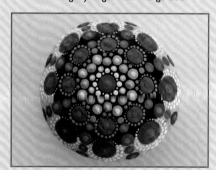

7 Use neon colors to add dots. Using the appropriately sized dotting tool, place a smaller dot on each of the dots, apart from the tiny rings and white dots. Put neon yellow on yellow dots, neon orange on orange, neon pink on red and in the center icon, and neon green on the blue. Place neon pink on the purple dots and for the largest purple dots, use a dot of non-neon lighter purple; once this has dried, add a tiny dot of neon pink.

8 Allow all paint to dry and apply 1–2 coats of protective finish before leaving to set for 24 hours.

Dream Galaxy

Create this unicorn silhouette on a galaxy stone and, when the lights go out, you'll be holding a little piece of magic right in your hands!

You will need:

- Stone
- Paint: black, white, neon pink, neon blue, neon yellow, and glow paint
- Paintbrush
- Pencil
- Masking tape
- Craft knife
- Small sponge
- Toothbrush
- Dotting tool
- Protective finish

1 Paint the entire top and sides of the stone with a black base coat. Allow this to dry, then add another coat of black paint.

2 In pencil, draw the outline of a unicorn in the center of the stone. Use masking tape to cover just the unicorn shape, cutting the tape carefully around the outline of the shape using a craft knife.

3 Using the sponge, dab a small amount of white paint across the stone and right over the masked-off unicorn outline, blending it so it's blurry.

4 Now, using the sponge, dab and blur neon pink paint over the top of the white. You don't need to wait for the paint to dry here.

5 Create depth in your galaxy by dabbing some black paint sparingly over the pink and white, to darken it along the sides. When the black paint dries, blur more neon pink over the top.

6 Continue to add colors to the galaxy with the sponge, using neon blue and neon yellow paint. Dab the blue paint to blend in with the pink for a purple haze, and blend yellow paint into the blue for a hint of green. There's no real map to the coloring: just try to keep the brightest area in the center, around the unicorn outline.

7 Use your glow paint to create stars! Dip the bristles of the toothbrush in glow paint, then hold the brush 2–3 in (5–7 cm) from the stone and run your finger across the bristles toward you. This will flick tiny bits of glow paint (stars!) at the stone. Add some larger stars with a dotting tool, then repeat the star splatter using white paint, to create stars that are visible in the daylight.

8 Using a paintbrush, add a thin layer of glow paint along the edge of the unicorn outline, and check your work in the dark. Add more stars if necessary. When all paint is dry, peel away the masking tape to reveal the unicorn silhouette! Touch up the unicorn's inside edges using black paint and let this dry as well. Finally, protect your star-studded dream stone with one or two coats of protective finish!

HANDY HINT

When checking your glow work, snap a photo of your stone while it's glowing to use as a reference for your edits when the lights are back on.

Pretty Paisley

There's just something perfect about paisley. It is a popular feather-shaped design motif that was based on an Indian pine-cone design that is continuously seen in the fashion world. Now you can reinvent it by applying it to your metallic rock art!

You will need:

- Oval-shaped stone approximately 2.7 in x 1.5 in (7 cm x 4 cm)
- Pencil
- Black permanent marker with extra-fine tip
- Metallic paint: gold, blue, purple
- Paintbrush: small
- Dotting tools: small
- Protective finish

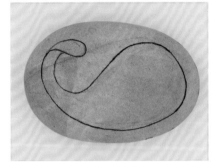

1 Draw the outline of a teardrop shape on the stone using pencil. When you're happy with it, go over it with black permanent marker.

2 Add the details inside the teardrop using a pencil, then trace over them with the black marker.

3 Using a black extra-fine-tipped permanent marker, draw the outline of a pointed fringe around the teardrop design. Then paint inside each shape with metallic gold and a small brush. Paint other sections of the design using gold, too.

4 Using a small brush, fill in more of the design with metallic blue paint, followed by metallic purple paint. When the paint has dried, add several additional coats, allowing the paint to dry in between layers. Touch up the black lines with a marker as you go.

5 Add the final, pretty paisley details, such as clusters of gold dots around the outside, contrasting colored dots and lines within the design, and a final touch-up wherever needed. When the paint is dry, coat the stone with protective finish.

HANDY HINT

Layering paint strategically can produce some really neat texture to the art once the stone is dry and the paint has cured. Adding more layers of one color than the others will make that part of the painted stone puff out, and adding extra layers of dots or lines will create bumps and ridges so that when handled, the stone is amazing to both see and touch!

Spiked Stone

You know that hardened acrylic paint that has sat out a bit too long or the chunks of paint you find on your lids? You could consider it a waste, only fit for the trash, or you could use it to turn your rocks into these spiked little curiosities!

You will need:

- Stone
- Dotting tools: small, medium, large
- Paintbrushes: medium, large
- Paint: black or navy, white
- Neon paint: pink, green, orange, yellow
- Protective finish

1 Paint a base coat. With a large round or flat brush, paint all visible parts of the stone using a dark shade of navy blue or black paint. Allow to dry and apply a second coat if needed. Allow to dry completely before moving on.

HANDY HINT

If you have a metallic paint color, try adding a few drops of silver to the navy or black base for a little shimmer!

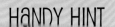

2 Use white paint to dot the design on the stone. This priming step may seem tedious, but it saves time and paint if you're using bright neon colors over a dark base. Start with the strip of dots down the center. Use a medium-sized dotting tool or round brush to place the largest dot at the center of the stone 0.2 in (5 mm). Continue dotting to the edge with slightly tapered dots that get smaller as they reach the ends. On either side of the center dotted line, add a line of small, close (without touching) dots from end to end. Allow all dots to dry.

3 On either side of the center lines, use a large dotting tool to place another large dot half way along the row of dots. Continue the row with large dots getting smaller towards each edge, keeping some space between them. Add a ring of tiny dots around each large dot. Space permitting, add another tapered row of large dots, circling each dot with a ring of tiny dots.

HANDY HINT

The process of tapering dots is used in some of the different activities in this book. Keep this term in mind as you'll see it again later!

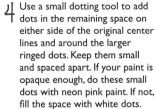

4 Use a small dotting tool to add dots in the remaining space on either side of the original center lines and around the larger ringed dots. Keep them small and spaced apart. If your paint is opaque enough, do these small dots with neon pink paint. If not, fill the space with white dots.

5 If you painted with white for the small dots in step 4, paint over the white with neon pink. Leave the dotted rings around the large dots as white, and also leave the small dotted lines that are on either side of the center line as white.

6 Paint the center row of dots neon green, leaving the small dots on either side white. Paint the next row of large dots on either side neon orange. Leave the ring of small dots white. Paint the last rows of large dots closest to the edges neon green. Start spiking the green and orange dots using thick paint. Saturate your small dotting tool well then dab it to the stone. Pull it up and off quickly, so the paint is pulled upward and stays raised. Do this a few times until a little spike forms. If your paint is thick enough to form a peak, then one or two coats should be enough. You do not need to allow the paint to dry completely, as having the paint not quite dry is helpful to the spiking process. When done, allow all paint to dry. Generally, the spikes will dry as you have left them but if they have receded while drying, apply another coat in the same manner and allow to dry again.

7 Top off all the green and orange spikes with a light dab of neon yellow. Be careful to dab lightly so as not to damage the spikes. While they are dry to touch, they are not yet cured and could potentially get knocked down. If the yellow does not appear very bright over the green and orange, prime the tips with white paint and allow to dry before painting over with yellow. Allow everything to dry for at least 1–2 hours.

HaNDY HINT

If your paint is not thick, you can thicken acrylic paint by leaving it exposed to air; allow some of the moisture to evaporate, but not so much that it dries out completely. Often artist or premium-brand acrylic paint is thicker than craft paint, or you can check under the lids of your paints for paint that has started to dry and is thicker than the rest. You can also use paints called 3-dimensional or puff paint for raised dots, which are sold in craft stores.

8 Apply 1–2 coats of finish and allow to dry for at least 24 hours to ensure the peaks stay strong. Once cured, the paint spikes are actually quite flexible and should bend and retain their form if pressed on.

Balance Cats

Create a happy balance with this adorable pair of intertwined kitties!
This stone makes a perfect little gift for the cat lovers in your life—
if you can bear to part with it, of course!

You will need:

- Pencil
- Drawing compass
- Stone
- Paint: white, black, and glow paint
- Large and small paintbrushes
- Protective finish

1 Using a pencil and drawing compass, draw a circle on your stone. Fill in the circle with white paint, and allow this to dry, then draw another, slightly smaller circle 1–2 mm inside the first. Paint over the border of the smaller circle with a thin black line.

2 Now, pencil in the kitty design: draw the tail of one cat at the bottom of the circle, coming from the left, and the tail of the other cat at the top of the circle, coming from the right.

3 Once you're happy with the tails, draw in the rest of the cats as shown. The paw of the right cat forms the neck area of the left cat and vice versa. Draw little hearts for the ears and noses, add lines for the closed eyes, and don't forget the whiskers. Cute!

4 Next, use a small brush and black paint to fill in the cat on the right-hand side, and paint the tail at the bottom black too. Once the paint has dried, use a fine paintbrush and white paint to go over the cat's eye, ear, nose, and whiskers. Paint the white cat's features in black.

5 When the paint is dry, coat all the white areas (including the black cat's facial features) with a thin layer of glow paint. Allow this to dry, then repeat the process once or twice more. Finally, charge the glow paint on the stone and turn out the lights to check for any areas that need extra glow. Refresh the black features of the white cat and touch up anywhere else that may need it. When all the paint is dry, cover your kitty creation with a coat or two of protective finish.

Triangled

This simple geometric design is all about perception. You may catch yourself wondering if this design is made up of lines between triangles, or triangles between lines! As you paint this rock, all kinds of shapes and patterns begin to emerge, depending on how you look at it.

You will need:

- Stone
- Painter's or masking tape
- Ruler
- Craft blade
- Cutting board
- Paintbrushes: small, large
- Paint: gray, white, blue, purple
- Neon paint: pink, yellow, green, orange
- Protective finish

1 First, cover your rock with a gray base coat using a large round or flat brush.

2 To create thin strips of tape, layer 6–8 pieces of tape (make these strips longer than the size of your stone) one on top of another. Very carefully, use a craft blade to cut very thin strips. It helps to use a ruler to keep the blade from slipping. Cut more than you need to get the best selection. It is tricky to get such small strips all evenly sized.

3 When you are finished, you should be able to peel the tape layers apart and have 6–8 strips of tape for each cut you make.

4 Next, lay a row of strips across the stone horizontally, parallel to one another, measuring about 0.4 in (1 cm) of space between each strip. Firmly press the edges of the strips to the stone so that little to no paint will be able to seep underneath when painted. Lay another row of parallel strips diagonally to the left over the top of the others, again with 0.4 in (1 cm) of space between them, making a diamond pattern. Lay a final row of strips, this time diagonally and to the right on top of the others. These strips should cross directly over the intersections of the other strips. Don't worry too much if your triangles are not exact in size; this can be adjusted later.

5 Ensure all tape is securely fixed to the stone, paying close attention to the intersecting areas or any areas where there are small indents, cracks, or holes. Use a larger brush or a sponge to cover the top of the stone in white paint as a primer, painting over the tape. Allow to dry and apply a second coat if needed.

6 When the white paint is completely dry, use whatever colors you like to paint the triangles. You can use all neon colors, or a mix of neon and regular paints.

7 Now comes the fun part! Carefully peel off the tape to reveal the design. Go strip by strip, removing the top layer first. Peel slowly: you don't want to peel up any paint that should remain stuck with the stone, Voila!

8 Because of a stone's uneven surface, it is likely you will have to fix up the outlines by going over any uneven lines with the stone color or filling in triangles with the appropriate color of paint. Use a small detail or liner brush. When complete, evenly coat the rock with 1–2 coats of protective finish.

HANDY HINT

The potential color combinations are endless: try a mix of both neon and regular colors, or just two or three neon colors throughout.

Proud Peacock Mandala

Is there anything more elegantly stunning than a peacock's feathers? The mix of bright greens and royal blues, their exquisite detail and delicacy? Who would have thought it could be replicated on a rock? You can proudly wow all your friends with this beautiful design.

You will need:

- Large stone, either round or square (about 4 in (10 cm) in diameter)
- Pencil
- Ruler
- Paint: dark navy blue, green, turquoise, gold, bronze, purple
- Metallic paint: golden green, turquoise blue, purple, blue, pink, dark green
- Paintbrush: small, medium, large
- Dotting tools: small, medium
- Black extra-fine tip permanent pen
- Protective finish

1 Use a pencil and ruler to draw a 3 × 3 in (75 × 75 mm) square or diamond shape across the top of the stone. Use a large brush to fill the square with dark blue paint. When the paint is dry, use your pencil to draw two more squares sized 2 × 2 in (50 × 50 mm) and 1.5 × 1.5 in (38 × 38 mm) within the first square. You can lightly draw horizontal, vertical, and diagonal lines through the center of the large square to help place the other squares inside, as well as to divide the squares into four: each of these sections will become a peacock feather "eye." Roughly outline the medium square with green and the small square with turquoise paint.

2 Fill each of the small center squares with matte turquoise-blue paint. As you paint around the points and edges of each square, extend them into the next square. Shape them approximately 0.2 in (5 mm) larger than their original size. Allow to dry, then do the same for the next square: fill it with matte green paint and round the edges, and extending it out slightly and into the currently bare stone. Finally, round the edges of the dark blue square. Ensure that all squares (or feathers) are about the same size and shape; it should resemble a stack of four-leaf clovers.

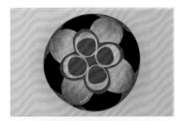

3 When the paint is dry, add additional coats for solid coverage. Paint over the green section with metallic golden-green paint. With your pencil, lightly add the details of the peacock feathers in the turquoise section. For each feather, draw an oval that almost fills the shape, leaving about 0.7–1.5 in (2–4 cm) of a border. Inside this, draw another smaller oval with a slightly flattened top. Using gold, paint the first oval outline in the small center feathers.

4 While the gold paint dries, continue painting the rest of the feathers. Within the flat-topped oval, draw a short, wide heart shape, closer to the flat top. Make the heart upside down, so its base points out to the edge of the stone. This is the pattern for all feathers: you can modify it to fit each section area. Begin to paint the rest of the colors, layering the colors and allowing them to dry in between. Allow time for each new section you've painted to dry before moving on to the next. Paint the remaining center feathers metallic turquoise blue with a matte turquoise border line left showing and dark navy blue for the hearts. Color the middle section of feathers bronze, then metallic purple.

5 While the paint dries, add contrasting colored border lines around the ovals where the paint is already dry. Paint a bright lime-green border around the bronze oval and another around the metallic blue oval in the center section. For the largest section of feathers, the outer-most ovals, the first oval is painted metallic blue.

6 Once the paint has dried, paint a matte bright lime-green circle inside the metallic blue in the large section. Add purple hearts inside the metallic purple middle section of feathers. Go around the outside of the middle section with navy blue border lines.

7 Paint metallic pink hearts in the green oval of the large outer feathers. Add purple borders around the ovals in the middle and outer sections and refresh any colored border lines that need it.

8 When the paint is all dry, go over the design to add details. Add small metallic dark green dots around the golden green oval and small lines with black pen inside the golden green of the mid-feathers. Draw medium-sized gold dots along the outside edge of the mid-feathers, small dots of matte green in the navy border of the large feathers, and small gold dots around the matte turquoise center feathers. Add dots of different colors inside the hearts. When the paint is dry, coat the stone with protective spray.

HaNDY HINT

Make your own golden peacock-green metallic paint by mixing metallic blue and gold paint together. Make this and any other new paint colors before beginning so that they are ready to use when the time comes. Store in a small, air-tight container to keep them from drying out.

Isometric Glow

Op-tickle your senses by creating this simple yet mind-bending optical illusion art design. It's much easier to produce than it looks!

You will need:

- Drawing compass
- Pencil
- Stone
- Ruler
- Paint: white, blue, yellow, and glow paint
- Large and small paintbrushes
- Protective finish

1 First, use a drawing compass to help you pencil in a large circle, centered on the stone. Then, begin to pencil the geometric design, starting by drawing six connected diamond shapes in the center of the circle. The diamonds should all have equal sides measuring about ½ in (1 cm).

2 Next, use a ruler to draw a ¾-in (2-cm) horizontal straight line going from the tip of the upper diamond to the right. Turn the stone and repeat this line from the next diamond tip, then do the same for the remaining diamond tips, turning the stone as you go. This will help you focus on one part at a time. Make sure you keep all the lines equal in length, evenly spaced, and aligned parallel with other lines on the same plane.

3 Continue the design by connecting another set of lines slanting downward, each measuring a little over ½ in (1.5 cm) long, and running parallel to the lines beside them.

4 From these lines, draw horizontal lines out to the circle's edge. Fill in the remaining lines as shown, then use a small, thin brush to paint over the pencil lines with white paint.

5 Once the paint has dried, use your larger brush to add a thin layer of white paint over the entire circle. This is your base coat; you should still be able to see your white painted lines through it.

6 Now add the color! Using one color at a time, paint all the shapes in the design, mixing yellow and blue to make the green. Try to leave a space between the colors so that the thin white outlines remain. Allow the paint to dry, then add additional coats if needed. Once you're happy with the colors and the paint has dried completely, refresh all the white outlines, including the circle outline.

7 Last, add one or two coats of glow paint on all the white lines—charge the glow to check whether any lines are uneven, and touch them up if needed. Let the glow paint dry before you protect your luminous op-art with a coat or two of protective finish.

HANDY HINT

Why not play around with mixing paint to create different shades? You can mix small amounts of blue into yellow paint to make a bright green, for example, and make colors paler by adding white paint.

Cosmic Tree

The Cosmic Tree symbol occurs in different cultures across the world, often with sacred meanings. Its roots plunge deep into the earth, and its branches reach high into the sky, so it is often seen as a representation of life itself: rooted in history, reaching up eternally to the future, and ever-changing. Keep this little tree displayed somewhere meaningful to you to keep yourself centered and inspire reflection.

You will need:

- Flat, round stone (approximately 2.5 in (6 cm) in diameter)
- Pencil
- Black fine-tip marker (optional)
- Paint: black
- Metallic paint: teal blue, purple, silver, gold
- Paintbrush: small, medium
- Dotting tools: small, medium
- Protective finish

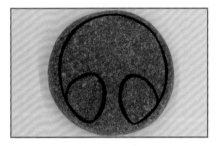

1 Using a pencil, draw a circle around the edge of the stone, but don't close it up: leave a 1 inch (2.5 cm) space at the bottom and continue the lines up into the circle and away from the center, stopping at the circle line. You should have two symmetrical oval shapes. This makes up the trunk of the tree. Trace over your pencil lines with a thin black marker.

2 Fill in the rest of the tree's branches by adding small leaf shapes through the center of the circle and symmetrically along both sides. Lightly form a full circle to make a border around the entire design at about 0.2–0.4 in (0.5–1 cm) from the stone's edge. Trace the shapes with black marker.

3 Paint the leaf shapes with metallic teal blue paint. Allow to dry, then paint another coat for extra coverage.

4 When the shapes are completely dry, use a pencil to draw swirling lines throughout each, then trace over these swirls with metallic purple paint using a small brush (please see the "Handy Hint" on the next page).

It can be difficult to clearly see your work with such metallic paints shining in your eyes. If you find this happening, tilt the stone in various directions until you find a spot where the glare is out of your eyes and you can clearly see your detailed handiwork.

5 Use a small brush to paint the entire tree with metallic silver paint. When the first coat has dried, add another coat and use a small dotting tool to dot small silver dots throughout the tree branches. Allow to dry. Use silver paint and a fine-tipped black marker to even up the lines and do touch-ups along the branches.

6 Paint silver around the outside of the circle and fill in the border. When the paint is dry, trace over the line edges with black marker. Add the final silver dots around the border and in the trunk, as well as gold star dots in the blue and purple sky. Leave to dry.

7 When the paint has dried, paint the outer edges of the stone purple. Add any final coats of color and outlines, then coat with protective spray.

Owl Friend

Tired of dotting? Paint a new owl friend! He looks like he may suffer from irritable owl syndrome, but don't let his scowl ruffle your feathers: he's a hoot and a solid friend for sure! Owl try to keep the puns to a minimum ...

You will need:

- Stone
- Pencil
- Paintbrushes: small, large
- Thin brush or black paint pen
- Paint: white, orange, black
- Neon paint: orange, yellow, pink, blue, green, purple
- Protective finish

HANDY HINT

Before beginning, draw or trace the outline of your stone on paper and practice your owl-making skills. Different-shaped stones may require small adjustments, but generally this design can work on just about any size or shape of stone, provided you have room for the eyes and wings. I have used a flattened egg-shaped stone with the larger end for the head and the narrower end for the body and wing area.

1 Use a large brush to prime your stone with 1–2 coats of white paint. Allow to dry. Lightly pencil the main outline of the owl on the stone. Draw the brow as a V shape about a third of the way down. Add the beak as a smaller V connected to the point of the brow. Lightly pencil in the eyes as partial circles connected to the brow on each side of the beak. Make sure they are the same size and evenly spaced. Draw the remaining V lines in the brow and continue forming the eyes. Shape another ring around the pupil and begin a third ring, but leave this unfinished, stopping just below the beak. Draw the wings coming inward from the edges of the stone to just before the center, curving downward and ending at the bottom. Finish drawing in the third eye circles, continuing the curved line from the brow on either side of the beak to the wing. At the edge of the stone, continue the curve of the line from the wing to the line. Add parallel lines connecting the middle eye circles closest to the beak.

2 Go over your outline for symmetry and adjust your lines with pencil and/or white paint if necessary. Adjust the outline using pencil and/or white paint as necessary. Once you have the outline of the owl's main features, begin painting. Paint the front area between the wings with orange paint, allow to dry, then add a coat of neon orange over top. This will darken the neon shade and make the other colors nearby appear brighter in contrast. Inside the iris circle, lightly pencil in the pupil. Leave a 0.2 in (5 mm) tapered space for the iris. Use a small round brush to paint the iris neon yellow, allow to dry, then paint in the pupil with black paint. Let all paint dry, during which time you can lightly pencil in 5–6 lines spanning off the second eye circle, crossing through the rings to the wing and outer edges of the stone.

3 Use a thin brush or paint pen to go over any pencil outlines. Use white paint to even out lines and fix any mistakes. Dry for 20 minutes or more; you want to be sure the black and white paint are dry before painting over the top.

7 In the lower portion of the wings, add in a thin black chevron detail within the green stripes. When the white paint is dry, carefully paint the wing dots neon pink, the front diamonds neon yellow, the brow dots neon purple in the yellow section, neon green in the blue section, and use neon orange for the top brow heart that falls over the edge. Finally, add a little white gleam in the black of the owl's eyes. Leave for 2–3 hours or more to ensure the paint is well set and dry.

4 Paint the brow's V lines: paint the largest neon pink, followed by neon yellow, then neon blue. Allow to dry. Use a pencil to lightly outline the detail of the wings. Draw a straight horizontal line across the top third of each wing. Below this, draw four or five vertical lines to form thick stripes. Use a small detail brush and begin to outline the top portion of the wing in black paint; trace alongside the inner top wing shape to leave a thin white border space between the shape (painted in purple with black outline) and the edge of the wing. While this is drying, paint the beak neon orange. While this dries, outline the lower portion of the wing with black and, when dry, use neon green and neon yellow paint for the stripes.

8 Apply 1–2 coats of protective finish and leave to cure for 24 hours.

5 While this dries, paint the little sections within the eye area. Beginning closest to the beak moving outward, paint the sections in the first ring neon orange, pink, and purple. Paint the next ring neon green, neon blue, and neon orange. The outer spaces to the side of the stone are painted neon green, blue, pink, and yellow.

6 Allow all paint to dry before adding a second coat or touch-up if needed. When the paint has completely dried (30–60 mins or more), use a small round brush and white paint to add the front diamond shapes and dots in the brow as well as across the purple part of the wings. In the blue top part of the brow, add another small V that extends over the edge of the stone into a heart shape. Apart from the dots, outline all the new white details in black once they are dry.

Glow Up

A layered, rainbow-colored mandala that shines from the inside, the white glowing background of this dotted design creates a very different, bright look!

You will need:

- Stone
- Paint: white, light purple, bright blue, blue, bright green, yellow, orange, pink, purple, and glow paint
- Paintbrush
- Dotting tools in a range of sizes from small to large
- Protective finish

HANDY HINT

With this design, when you fix mistakes, don't forget to make sure the glow coat underneath is still uniform with the rest. Add more glow paint if need be!

1 Start by painting a base coat over the visible area of the stone, using two coats of white paint. When this is dry, paint two or three layers of glow paint over the white, allowing time to dry between each one. Charge the paint and check to make sure you have a good, even glow before you go on to the next step.

2 Use a large dotting tool to make the center dot in light purple paint, then surround this with tiny, evenly spaced dots in the same color.

3 Add the next ring of dots using bright blue paint. Position these dots between each dot of the first ring, lined up exactly below the spaces. Now, continue dotting the entire stone in this alternating dot pattern. As you span out with each new ring, gradually increase the size of the dots to cover the stone.

4 On my stone, the next two rings of dots are blue, then there are three rings of bright green, followed by one ring each of bright yellow, orange, pink, purple, blue, and back to green and bright yellow—repeating until the top and sides of the stone are covered. Add a large purple dot in the center of the stone.

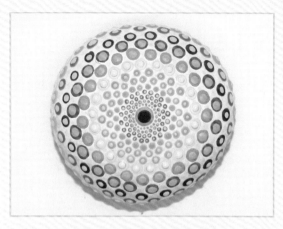

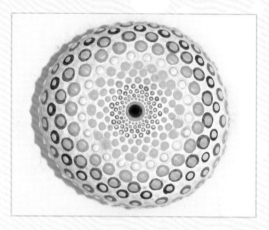

5 When all the paint has dried, add a second coat if needed. Then, begin to add new dots over each colored dot in a slightly smaller size, using a lighter shade of the same color, made by mixing a little white paint into the color.

6 Add a darker dot of purple to the center dot, inside the lighter purple dot. To finish, add tiny dots of glow paint in the spaces between each of the colored dots to give you maximum effect when the lights go out! When all the paint is dry, protect your art with one or two coats of protective finish.

Rock Garden

"If I had a flower for every time I thought of you, I could walk through my garden forever." Make a flower for your forever garden. These pretty posies are just the perfect flower: they stay in bloom all year, need no care, and never wilt! This concentric design can be created using as many different colors and details as you can imagine.

You will need:

- Stone
- Pencil
- Dotting tools: small, medium, large
- Paintbrushes: small, large
- Thin brush or white and black paint pens (both optional)
- Paint: white, black, red, light pink
- Neon paint: pink, yellow
- Protective finish

1 Use a large round brush to paint a white circle or oval on top of the stone. Leave some space around the edges. When the paint has dried, lightly pencil a flower. Begin the outline in the center of the stone. Pencil in a small dot and add larger circles around it. From this circle, there will be many thin lines spanning out around it, but don't draw them yet. Rather, where the lines will end, lightly pencil in another circle. Begin to form the first petals—small rounded bumps all the way around the circle, like a cloud shape.

2 Begin painting the flower. Fill in the cloud shape with a small round brush and black paint. Allow the black paint to dry completely and apply a second coat if needed. Pencil in another ring of larger bumpy petals, about twice the size of the previous ones. Stagger these petals in relation to the last by starting and finishing each new petal bump at the top and center of the black bumps beneath. Finish the flower outline by using white paint and adding a third ring of staggered bumpy petals along the outer edges of the oval base. Make them larger than those before it.

3 Use a small round detail brush or extra-fine-tip paint pen to outline the remainder of the flower petals in black. Leave a thin outline of white around the entire flower.

4 In the middle of the black petal area, use a small round brush and red paint to form a circle in the center of the flower. Let the red paint dry completely then use a dotting tool to place a dot in the center with black paint. Make this small enough to leave the edge of the red exposed, but large enough to fit another dot inside it. When the black paint has dried, add a white dot just large enough that the black slightly shows as an outline around it. Dot a small ring inside the red circle with white paint.

5 Use a thin detail brush and white paint or an extra-fine white paint pen to add lots of thin white lines extending out from the red circle to where the black petals begin. Do this all the way around, placing a tiny white dot on the end of each thin line. Use black paint to thin out and neaten any white lines as well as outline around the red circle.

6 Paint in all the petals with a small brush and neon pink paint, leaving a small space of white outline between the pink paint and the petals of the ring before. Once the pink paint has dried, use white paint (pen or brush) over the top of any pink to create a nice even outline around each petal. Allow all paint to dry. Apply more coats if needed, drying completely between each coat. With a small round brush, add stripes to the outer ring of petals with light pink paint (not neon). Once all paint has completely dried, go over the outlines with black and white paint to make them sharper and cleaner. Use an extra-small round detail brush or paint pen to clean up the outlines within the design, including the center dot, the red dot, and each black petal outline. Clean up the white outline around the petals and the entire flower.

7 Add in the petal detailing. In the second ring of petals, form a thin curved black line inside each petal over the pink paint. Add another coat of neon pink in the border formed by the black line. Then add a little black sprout ending in a dot in the middle of each petal, and use a small dotting tool to add a neon yellow dot in the center of each one, leaving a black outline. In the outer ring of petals, thinly outline each stripe. Allow all paint to dry and go over any mistakes using the color of paint you use as an "eraser."

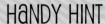

HaNDY HINT

Brush strokes tend to thin out the neon paint, making it more translucent and leading to streaks. Apply thin coats and let them dry completely before applying a new coat. If it is a small area, try dabbing paint on instead of using brush strokes.

8 When all paint is dry, spray with 1–2 coats of finishing spray and leave it to dry overnight.

Mermaid Moment

Ah, the life of a mermaid: all bubbles and no troubles! Take a moment to make this daydream a reality by creating this glowing design on stone.

You will need:

- Pencil
- Drawing compass
- Stone
- Paint: white, light blue, blue, yellow, black, bright pink, and glow paint
- Fine-tipped paintbrush
- Small paintbrush
- Protective finish

1 Use a drawing compass to pencil in a circle, off-center in the upper part of the stone. The circle needs to fit the mermaid, while leaving room for her tail outside the circle. Draw two or three smaller circles on the upper edge for the bubbles, then fill in the circles with white paint for a base coat. Paint a thin white line around the main circle.

2 Add thin white borders around the bubbles. When the white paint is dry, use pencil to lightly draw the figure of a mermaid sitting inside the large circle, with her tail extending out into the stone. Paint the background and bubbles light blue and use white paint to prime the mermaid.

3 Paint the main colors of the mermaid, starting with the tail. Color the entire tail blue, with an emphasis along the edges. Allow this to dry, then paint yellow down the middle of the tail, blending it out to the edges to create a bright yellow-green shading.

4 Paint her hair yellow, then add streaks of white paint over the top. While you're at it, add a very light yellow tinge to the skin as well.

5 Using a fine-tipped paintbrush, add a thin outline in black paint between the different colors used on the mermaid, and mark in the facial features and other details. Use white paint to help contour the black outlines and even them up where necessary.

6 Use the small paintbrush to add bright pink streaks to the hair and around the tail fin. Apply small amounts at a time and blend with the other colors to create orange and purple. Add a bit of pink color to the cheeks, lips, shell bikini, and star hair ornament. Add orange dots to the star hair ornament.

7 Add the final small details: yellow dots on top of the orange in the star, and pink and yellow dots in the tail. Touch up the black outlines and add more streaks in her hair. Try to make sure everything looks the way you want it before you add the glow paint.

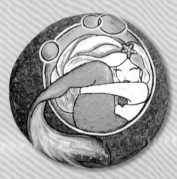

8 Now it's time to make your mermaid glow! Using a small paintbrush, add long lines of glow paint through the hair and tail fin, beginning in the center and working outward. Paint scales throughout the tail, and add thick lines of glow paint over the white outline of the circle border and bubbles. Highlight the star hair ornament and shell bikini with glow paint. Check the glow in darkness and make any adjustments needed.

9 When the paint is dry, cover your mer-mazing rock art with one or two coats of protective finish, and position your mermaid wherever you want a magical reminder of the sea—and its phosphorescence!

HANDY HINT

Be creative! Why not try adding metallic paint, sparkles, sequins, or tiny shells and other treasures found at the beach to decorate your mermaid and make her unique?

Golden Pyramid

Pyramids are magnificent and mysterious structures that have their origins in ancient times but that still impress us today. Now you have the same effect with this striking golden-pyramid design. It radiates power and style!

You will need:

- Round stone (about 2.5 in (6 cm) in diameter)
- Pencil
- Compass
- Paint: black, yellow, gold, pearl white, orange, red, bright red
- Metallic paint: blue, light yellow, purple
- Paintbrush: small, medium
- Dotting tools: small, medium, large
- Protective finish

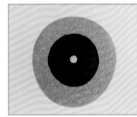

1 Form a large, 1 in (3 cm) dot that takes up about half of the space in the center of the stone. Fill the circle with black paint using a medium brush. When the paint has dried, use a medium-sized dotting tool and metallic blue paint to add a 0.2 in (5 mm) dot in the center of the black circle.

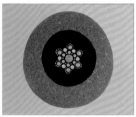

2 Use a small dotting tool and bright yellow paint to evenly place six small dots of equal size about 0.6 in (1.5 cm) around the blue center icon. On a clock, these would be at 12, 2, 4, 6, 8 and 10 o'clock. Carefully add 0.4 in (1 cm) or smaller dots of metallic blue between each of the bright yellow dots. Try to make sure you don't touch any of the existing dots as you make more dots. Continue to move out from the center icon. Place another ring of six metallic light-yellow dots that are 0.8 in (2 cm): just slightly larger than the bright yellow dots in the previous ring. Add some tiny blue dots between them.

3 For the dots in the next ring, make them the same size but use gold paint. Place these gold dots in line with the bright yellow dots. Leave a bit more space between the gold dots and those around them so that you can add a ring of tiny 0.2 in (0.5 cm) metallic pearl white dots around each of the gold dots individually.

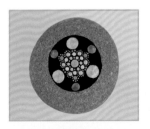

4 At 12, 4, and 8 on a clock, add two tiny dots of bright orange, side by side. In the remaining three spaces, add small bright orange dots, spacing them so that you can fit a ring of tiny gold dots around each. The dots should combine to form a triangular shape. Use a large dotting tool to make three large 0.3 in (8 mm) dots of gold just above the two small orange dots. Make these gold dots large enough to just touch the edge of the black circle. Add three medium size 0.2 in (5 mm) metallic purple dots in line with the gold-circled bright orange dots.

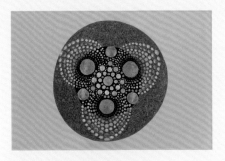

5 Focus your attention on the large gold dots. Begin to add rings of dots that slightly increase in size with each new ring. The first ring is made of tiny red dots, followed by bright red, bright orange, bright yellow, metallic pastel yellow, gold, and finally metallic white pearl. As you add the rings, you will need to slightly reduce the size of the dots. Add a couple of metallic blue dots to fill in the corners next to the metallic purple dots.

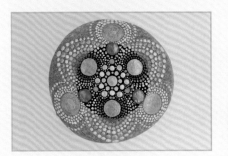

6 Use a small paintbrush to make three extra-large 0.4 in (1 cm) gold dots in line with the metallic purple dots. Add rings of tiny dots of yellow, gold, and metallic white pearl. These rings should wrap around the side of the stone.

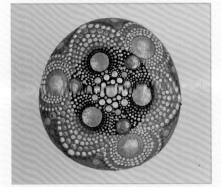

7 Add metallic blue dots in the corners where the white pearl dots meet. Create a ring of small metallic purple dots surrounding the entire design. Add finishing touches, like a second coat of paint anywhere that it is needed. When all is dry, add 1–2 coats of protective finish.

HANDY HINT

Mix and mingle! Use different types of paint such as matte and neon in your designs and highlight them using shimmering metallics.

Enchanted Urchin Amulet

You will feel like a spirit of the sea with this amazing radiating-dot design.
The metallic colors will glisten and shimmer as if they are rippling under the waves;
this rock never fails to impress!

You will need:

- Small round stone — 2 in (5 cm)
- Paint: navy, violet, metallic white pearl
- Metallic paint: blue, gold, purple, rose gold
- Paintbrush: small, medium
- Dotting tools: small, medium, large
- Protective finish

1 Paint the base coat with matte navy and matte violet. Paint the colors in alternating star shapes with five-part symmetry.

2 Use a large dotting tool and white pearl paint to make a 0.1 in (3–4 mm) dot in the center of the stone; use a small dotting tool to make 10 tiny dots around the large one. Try to keep them all the same size (0.04 in/1 mm) and line them up with the edges where one base color meets the next.

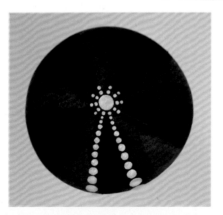

3 Continue to use white pearl paint and begin to add small dots in line with the center dots that span out to the edge of the stone. Increase the size of the dots as they move outward so that the dots on the edge of the stone are as large as the center icon.

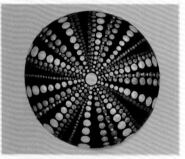

4 Use a small dotting tool to make more lines of dots that span out from the center icon. Create lines of small metallic blue dots after every second pearl line. Unlike the pearl white dots, keep your metallic blue dots tiny all the way to the outer edge of the stone.

5 Add 5 lines of gold medium-size dots 0.08 in (2 mm) down the middle of each violet base color. The gold dots should get slightly larger as they move out from the middle of the rock.

6 Continue adding lines of colored dots that span out from the center icon. As the available space begins to fill up, taper the dots closest to the center icon and increase their size (if desired) as you span toward the stone's edge. Add rows of purple dots and rows of dots of rose gold (formed by mixing metallic purple and gold). Next to the existing rows of gold dots, add lines made up of small metallic blue and tiny gold dots.

7 Make any final touch-ups and when the stone has dried, cover with protective finish. If adding a gem in the center for some extra sparkle, apply it once the finish has been applied and is dry.

HaNDY HINT

If you are using a gemstone in the center of the urchin, make sure that your first center dot is about the same size as the gem you will use. If it's too large, it will show under the gem and if it's too small, you will be cutting off the dots that surround the center when the gem is applied at the very end.

Fantastic Fungi

Did you know there are real-life mushrooms, snails and other living organisms that glow in the dark? It's called "bioluminescence"! In this project, you'll paint your very own bioluminescence-inspired marvelous mushroom scene!

You will need:

- Stone
- Large and small paintbrushes
- Paint: white, black, neon blue, neon yellow, neon red, neon green, neon orange, and glow paint
- Pencil
- Small dotting tool
- Protective finish

HANDY HINT

Not confident in your drawing skills? Carbon transfer paper (available from craft and stationery stores) is your friend! Just print out a royalty-free picture you love, tape the printout to your stone with some transfer paper underneath, then trace the outlines with a pencil. Voilà— they're magically transferred to the stone!

1 Using your bigger paintbrush, paint a large white oval base coat over the center of your stone. Leave approximately ½–¾ in (1–2 cm) of bare stone as a border. Allow to dry, then add another coat for good coverage.

2 Use a pencil to lightly draw in the mushroom scene. If any parts of your drawing go beyond the white oval onto the bare stone, use white paint to fill these areas.

3 Use a small, thin brush and black paint to trace over the main outline of your sketch, then outline the black dots on the mushroom caps as well. You can tidy up any mistakes or uneven lines by using white paint as an "eraser."

4 Now, paint in your colors! Begin by painting the background neon blue, then paint the tops of the mushrooms neon red and the underside of the caps neon yellow. Leave the bottom edge of the caps and the dots white. Paint any grass neon green.

5 Paint the snail's body neon orange with yellow dots throughout. Paint its shell neon yellow, then allow the stone to dry. Using your thin brush or a dotting tool, add glow paint to the white dots and white rims of the mushroom caps. Then, apply a single, thick coating of glow paint over the lower parts of the two mushroom stems at the front of the scene. While the glow paint is still wet, use the thin brush to paint horizontal stripes of white paint over the top, then immediately use a clean thin brush or a dotting tool to drag lines through the stripes from top to bottom. This will create a swirl pattern.

6 Repeat the technique in step 5 on the snail shell, to create swirls of glow and white paint. When the paint dries, the glow will appear yellow in daylight.

7 Paint lines of glow underneath the mushroom caps, and add some "rays" of glow to the blue background by painting vertical lines of glow paint on it. Add some glow paint to the snail's body, the grass blades and the remaining mushroom stems. Add some neon yellow to the fringed rings that sit at the top of each mushroom stem. Charge the glow under a light, then check in the darkness whether you need to make any adjustments or add more coats of paint. Once you're happy with it, retouch the black outlines and allow all paint to dry overnight before adding a coat or two of protective finish.

Infinity Stone

Behold your very own hand-held galaxy! This design is amazingly simple. You won't need any special tools to form this swirling design. Once you start the pattern, you will see the spiral naturally emerge from the placement of dots that increase in size with each new ring. Adding color sends you spiralling off into infinity!

You will need:

- Stone
- Dotting tools: small, medium, large
- Paintbrushes: large
- Paint: black, white, light blue, mid-blue, dark blue
- Neon paint: purple, pink, yellow, blue
- Protective finish

1 Use a relatively flat stone so that you have space to expand out the spiral formation. A round shape is not necessary but does add to the symmetry of the design. Choose a stone that is at least 2 in (5 cm) across, as you will need room on the stone for the center dot and spiral. Use a large brush and paint over the whole stone using a black base color. Allow to dry.

2 Prime the dot design using white paint and your dotting tool of choice. Place a dot of about 0.3 in (8 mm) in diameter in the center of the stone. This dot needs to be large enough to fit 24 tiny dots, evenly spaced around it without touching.

3 Once you have your center icon surrounded by 24 evenly spaced, tiny dots, the rest of the design is fairly easy. Begin the next ring of dots, staggered so that they are above the spaces between the previous dots of the ring. Make them slightly larger than the last ring. Do not sink them into the space: just align them as a new ring.

HANDY HINT

Practice this dot design on paper beforehand so you get the hang of how it works. Experiment with using different colors if you wish.

4 Continue adding rings of dots, making each one larger than the previous ring. Don't rush! Alignment, as well as gradually increasing in dot size with each new ring, is key to making this design. It is important to turn the stone as you dot to get the best dot alignment possible.

HANDY HINT

The number of dots is important as it determines the number of colors you can use for the swirls. Having an even number allows for equal color distribution. With 24, there are six sections, each with four different colors: one shade of purple followed by three shades of blue.

5 Continue adding rings of dots until you have covered the stone to the edge, spilling over the side if possible. Finish the design by tapering the dots down in size for the last few rings that reach over the sides and under the stone. Allow all dots to dry, then hold the stone away from you to get a different perspective. This view allows you to see if any dots could use a touch-up so they're a bit larger or smaller, or if they need adjusting to be better aligned.

6 Paint with color. Use three shades of blue (light blue, mid-blue, dark blue) and bright neon purple. Whatever colors you use, keep them in the same order from start to finish. Start by painting the smallest dots around the center icon. Begin with purple, followed by light blue, mid-blue, and dark blue in that order. Repeat the color pattern until the ring is complete.

7 For the next ring, move the color pattern one dot over, going in a counterclockwise direction. Beginning again with purple, place the dot above and to the right of the same color dot in the ring before it. Continue to paint the colors in the same order, changing color dot by dot for at least the first 3–4 rings, until you can clearly see where each color is curving away from the center.

8 Now you can save time by finishing each color one at a time, row by row (i.e. all purple dots, then all light blue, and so on), rather than alternating colors dot by dot, one ring at a time. Allow all paint to dry and apply the second coating if needed.

9 Paint the center icon dark blue. Go over the blue and purple dots with a slightly lighter color. Add a tiny dot of neon pink on the purple, neon blue on the mid-blue, mid-blue on the dark blue, and finally a very light blue on the light blue.

10 To finish, add some bright stars to this galaxy. Use your small dotting tool to make tiny neon yellow dots in all the little spaces around each dot. Do this as far up from the sides toward the center as you can fit, without touching other dots. Add a smaller dot of mid-blue to the center dot and top it with a tiny dot of light blue, allowing each to dry between coats.

11 Do any touch-ups or second coatings and when all paint is dry, apply one or two coats of protective finish and leave to dry for 24 hours.

Congratulations!

By following the steps in this book, you have forged some fantastic pieces of rock art. What will you do with your little creations now? First of all, you can have a photoshoot to capture your brilliant new creations. Then you could then take your art to the internet! You will find communities of other artists who love to paint stones, and you could be inspired to come up with new ideas of your own.

Get inspired and continue your rock-painting journey. You do not have to look far for ideas; they are everywhere. From a flower in the garden to the shape of a snowflake, inspiration is never more than a stone's throw away.

I hope you have enjoyed using metallic, neon, and glow-in-the-dark paints in your art. Now keep on shining, and always remember to think happy dots!

A note on the author

Katie Cameron lives and creates in Halifax, Nova Scotia, on Canada's east coast. Katie is a self-taught rock-artist who, when not in her studio, can be found strolling along the coastline looking for the next #Hfxrocks art inspiration.